The Economist

Conclusions on politics, society, and economics

July 27, 2006 through January 13, 2007

Scott Hallal-Negishi

July 27, 2006

Energy, economy, Sudan, Pakistan, India, United States of America, guns, battle, war, raging war. The international limelight is now on. The world is certainly in turmoil. Pakistan is right in the middle of two countries, India and Afghanistan, which is causing great turmoil in all three countries. Landmines and fences are being placed on the border of Afghanistan and Pakistan. Bombs and missiles are being sent from Pakistan into India and from India into Pakistan. Trains are blowing up. People are being killed. America is helping India because they support India. India seems to be supporting America. The great tie between the two has something to do with democracy, Christianity, and nuclear arms. Nuclear energy as some say. Russia is a growing power. They are turning away from democracy, which is worrying America. But I support Russia. They are strong and fierce and smart. They will rise once again. They will devour America along with China. Meaning, with the help of China, Russia will devour America. But, hopefully this will never be. Hopefully, America can keep peace. Hopefully, China can keep peace. Hopefully, Russia can keep peace. And Europe grows. They will unite. They are uniting. The only thing they need is one great leader to join them in power. But, hopefully, they never crave power. Hopefully, they do not need to squander the world. To conquer the world. They have already done that. They have learned their lesson.

The world is doing a make-over. Every country wishes to grow and develop. Although, when I say every country, I mean only those that are active in world politics and that are mentioned in The Economist Magazine. The other countries are keeping to themselves and that is the way they like it. Or so I suppose.

The G8 Summit meeting in Russia. Mr. Putin would have been proud. Mr. Putin won the meeting. He was the honorary guest. He was the host.

July 29, 2006

The economic world is coming into view. Japan, the United States of America, Iran, Russia, Europe, Spain, India, Pakistan, China, Asia, Canada, Mexico, Africa, and all of the rest. The map of the world is also coming into view, geographically speaking. I am beginning to see the world. The world is coming alive. I cannot say much as of yet, but that will come on its own accord. For now, I just want to substantiate my voice. I wish to build my own opinion and let that opinion carry weight within this world. My interest in economics is starting to develop. I wish to know more about Japanese economics and Russian economics. I wish to know how different economies in different countries work together and compete against one another.

My current understanding of Japan is that of its women. I have spoken with Japanese women who have traveled to Hawaii in order to escape the social restrictions of their country. As women, they must follow the traditional order bestowed upon them by the men who are leaders of companies. The women must follow certain social roles even if they do not wish to follow them. These women come to Hawaii to escape it all. These women wish to learn and speak. They wish to go out to parties at night. They wish to be human beings with thoughts and feelings of their own. These women are living largely, as an American may think. Large. They are living how they wish to live. They join together with other women to live as such. To be strong. The men of America are perhaps accepting of these powerful women. On July 14, 2006, the Bank of Japan raised its interest rates from 0.00% to 0.25%. The Japanese feel confident in their economy once again. I read that in the past, maybe within the past twenty years, the banks had raised the interest rates to 6.00%, but it had caused the banks to collapse back to 0.00% when mixed into the economics of the world. Something always happens to slow down the growth of a country. Something also always happens to improve the decay of a country. The world is up and down. Always up and down. Never satisfied. Never staying the same. And I do realize that I say this knowing many people do not think this way and many countries do not think in this manner, but for those countries that choose to enroll and take part in the world economy, that is how it works. I am very interested in what will happen to America's economy. I am beginning to see a fall down, however little it may be.

August 2, 2006

The future of globalisation. The future of globalisation? A global trade.
World Trade Organization. The world is fending for itself. For
themselves. Each country has a stake to claim. America will not budge.
India will not sacrifice. Europe is staying strong. Nobody wants to
compromise. So then what? DOHA will fade just as its predecessor did in
Brussels. Geneva will not last. Countries must protect their people.
Trade must go on but with enough tariff incentive to build a strong
economy. Just because America outsources most of its money earned
through taxes does not mean every country can do that. America does
have the advantage because they do not invest in its people and are
more concerned with holding power in the world at large, but even
though they do does not mean other countries do not see them doing
that. What about America? What about the people? Welfare to Work.
Why worry so much about the outside world when you have yet to
solve the problems of your own people? I realize America must hold
strong. They have much cause and much to hold onto. They must keep
their power because they are not the only ones relying upon their
strength. Many other countries rely upon America's position. Economy
rules the world. Education prices are going up while education quality is
going down. Capitalism is taking hold of education. People are being
numbed through media. Retirement has been dissolved. Unions have all
collapsed or are soon to be extinct. Everyone is on their own. Socialism
is not even a glimpse. Medical is nonexistent. The elderly are being
swept into homes and communities of their own. The past is being
eliminated. Only the future exists.

I fear for the children. I fear for their innocence and susceptibility to the ideas that are being created in media. One example is time through the past. The idea of how old history is. In a movie the characters became shocked and astounded upon looking at the old and ancient document – The U.S. Constitution. How old is the Constitution? Children will begin to think 300 years is a long time ago. This is a fear of mine. If I can see the changes taking place, but I see them for entertainment, then they will surely exist as fact to those children who do not know any better.

August 9, 2006

The war between Israel and Hizbullah continues. Israel has struck the town of Qana in Lebanon killing at least 28 people including more than half of them children. This will definitely dampen the peace keeping negotiations and weaken the opportunity of a ceasefire on both sides. America is taking on the side of Israel supposedly and France may be taking on the side of Lebanon as they have been involved with Lebanon on many issues in the past. America sides with Israel for purposes that could lead beyond just helping their friend. Some say this is a war involving Iran and the United States even if Israel and Hizbullah are doing the fighting.

After 47 years ruling Cuba, Fidel Castro has temporarily passed power over to his 5-year younger brother because of the surgery he must have done. This is big news for the United States as the United States has had shaky relations with Cuba because of the Communist government Castro has implemented. The United States has had a trade and economic embargo with Cuba since the early 1960s. Some say this has affected, to an almost destructive point, Cuba's economy.

A point of view has struck me recently. The middle class of America may be less educated than the middle class of Europe. The middle class of America is very important because it carries the majority of the people. The middle class does not rule but the middle class does rule consumption. And consumption is the most definite point of America that carries this country. The middle class can tilt an issue. The middle class can also carry the propaganda that it is fed through media without necessarily questioning its validity. America has certain attributes when dealing with international affairs. One of those issues is the stance America takes with war and fighting. America is quick to act. The biggest values these days seem to be democracy and freedom. America was quick to act with Iraq. All of a sudden Hussein, Saddam had been captured, of which he is currently being held on trial for humanity crimes. Crimes against humanity. The U.S. acts fast. Whereas in Europe, they think more closely about the consequences and their history before acting.

August 10, 2006

Congo, fair Congo. Congo has nearly successfully completed its first democratic election voted upon by the people in over 40 years. 45 I think. Maybe 47. Some minor challenges arose much like anything else, but overall the election will be a success.

Georgia seems to be an interesting country. Located under Russia touching Turkey, Georgia is a very happening country. Georgia. Georgia. Oh, fair Georgia.

Africa. South Africa. South Africa is a place of its own. Located directly below Africa, a part of Africa. Africa Unite. South Africa. I do not know much about South Africa. South Africa is ...

Australia. Supposedly Australia has a high crime rate. I do not know much beyond that.

I do not know much today.

Oh well...

August 13, 2006

Wal-Mart. This week's Economist shed an article on Wal-Mart in Germany: that Wal-Mart was forced to close some of its stores in Germany. The failure of Wal-Mart in Germany is said to be closely related to the cultural differences in Germany as compared to the Wal-Mart mentality springing from America. Germans just don't take to the pushy sales oriented bargains of Wal-Mart. Wal-Mart was more of an American identity than simply a store selling things. Wal-Mart chose to orient its store more in English than in German. Who is going to be the communicator when the top executive in Germany does not even speak German? Germans just don't buy the whole Wal-Mart thing without thinking it over first. Germans are very logical. They have rules that they follow for reasons that are right and just to them. The rules are there for a reason. Then Wal-Mart comes along and tries to do its own thing thinking humans are susceptible to the imaginaries of their ways. Wal-Mart is also hitting sore spots in South Korea and even in Japan. The near future may see more closings for Wal-Mart. They are still growing however. But, because Wal-Mart, like most American companies, relies upon growth, the moment they stop growing is the moment they fail. Wal-Mart will most definitely see itself in a hole someday. Now is the time for change. People are changing. Wal-Mart will see itself winning for only a limited amount of time. They will come off of the planet just as they came on. Little by little, the dynasty will die. Wal-Mart is just one of the many American dynasties to roam the earth. America is the great land of ups and downs. The world is now a part of that great American tradition.

August 20, 2006

Many countries are being faced with an unstoppable change in education that must be addressed. In China, existing schools and organizations with enough money are creating themselves as a private school entity in order to make more money than being classified as a public school. For organizations that are not existing schools, the creation of a private school is a business tactic in order to receive tuition compensation. More and more students are finding the benefits of having a degree from a prestigious university. Schools are making money on their wants and desires, which have been implanted by schools and through globalization.

In Britain, schools are facing the challenge of keeping grade levels down to a level that will distinguish students as being highly intelligent and just bright.

In America, the grade is highly looked upon when it is viewed as a G.P.A. (Grade Point Average). But getting the A does not distinguish an individual whatsoever. An A will be handed out for simply following the clearly set-out directions the teacher hands out to the students through a course syllabus at the beginning of the year. An A can easily be obtained through effort, not through intelligence, which seems contradictory. I understand by putting in effort, one may become more intelligent or by working hard, an intelligent person will be able to perform; however, one can easily obtain an A in every class of his collegiate career by simply doing as the teacher says and never putting in a voice of his or her own once. The A is merely a form of time and conformity. Testing is a good way to appropiate grades. One cannot maneuver his or her way to an A grade without answering the questions correctly. Yet tests, or are tests a good way to judge intelligence? Yes and No. I guess it matters who or what is administering the test and who was the one who created the questions. Tests can be viewed as another form of conformity in one sense. Conformity to the people who created the test. And not that conformity is a bad thing. Conformity is a great way to pass along knowledge and tradition.

August 26, 2006

On August 14, the war between Lebanon (Hizbullah) and Israel was put to a cease fire. The cease fire is taken in many different ways according to what views an individual or a country has. Hizbullah is taking the ceasefire as a bit of a win. However, Israel is still intruding into their territory, but over the next few months, if the ceasefire holds, Israel will move their soldiers back. Israel is also taking the ceasefire as a win, only in my view, they see it as less of a win as does Hizbullah see a win. If the fighting stopped then I see the ceasefire as a win. Politically and culturally the ceasefire seems to be only a stand still which will lead to more fighting. The reason for the war may be ambiguous and based on feelings of nationalism and those differences have not been brought to a compromise. Communication lacks. The strife and problems still exist. Nothing has been accomplished. The two parties are still in the same predicament as they were prior to the war. It is the same predicament which goes on and on in not only their countries but all around the world. It is this lack of communication that leads to war and greater wars with much higher consequences. I can see where this strife is headed. Surely, if this ceasefire holds, it will only be a hold. Perhaps, just as I read about past battles and disputes that happened thirty and even forty years ago, in twenty years or thirty years, or even fifty years, I will see this dispute arise again. I will then look back upon the battle between Hizbullah and Israel in August of 2006 and know that without proper communication and proper conclusion, the events will always return. Those events of violence and battle.

There seems to be much controversy over the Israel matter. Nations and individuals see Israel in many different ways. Does Israel have the right to exist as a nation? Israel was born out of World War Two. It is a nation born to house those Jewish peoples who suffered and were outcast during the great catastrophes which haunted the entire world during World War Two. The elimination of Jewish people. Because the Jewish did not have many places to go after the war ended because they were not so welcome in most parts of Europe, a state was created for them supported by the United States. The United States therefore has great links to Israel. They helped mold and shape the State. America must now carry Israel or at least follow behind Israel supporting their moves. Hizbullah is supported by Iran. Iran funds Hizbullah's party. Lebanon is not a state run by Hizbullah. Hizbullah is more of a figure of the people. Lebanon is politically run by Mr. Siniora, a prime minister. His position is rather awkward and under pressure in connection to Hizbullah. He was forced in a certain respect to express the ceasefire and accordingly win by Hizbullah as a win for Lebanon. He must support the win as a factor of national pride, but in a way Hizbullah is taking power from him by taking people and money from Iran to run in a direction of its own that does not, as far as I know, take orders from Mr. Siniora. This is by far a strange situation that I have learned is similar to many other situations in the past.

September 2, 2006

Iran could be the next big player of global dominance. Iran is currently exerting its influence on many global situations that involve global dominance. They are financing sides in war and they are taking a stance on their own nuclear usage. They are saying that they too have the right to develop nuclear technology and use it for energy purposes and to use as a developing country. The world is saying No. Iran may not have the ambitions to gain global dominance, but surely they will continue to grow and continue to act as a key component of the political world. Globalisation is now here. This is the globalisation of economics, industry, and natural resources. Iran can take part in this developing global infrastructure.

September 6, 2006

My voice is growing. Surely it is. Europe. Europe is becoming a grand
and eloquent force. The European entity is growing large. The union of
countries within Europe. This means Europe is growing. Countries are
coming together under one currency, under one political structure,
under one supreme goal. Or, if this has not happened already
completely, it seems to be heading into that direction. My stance is
strong: that Europe is growing strong. That it is growing indefinitely, but
under unsuspicious eyes. Europe is quietly growing. It is doing it in its
own way. Europe is becoming a self. China is heading into the direction
of global dominance as well. It is slowly but surely taking over the world.
It moves slow so as not to alarm anyone. It is moving though. It is surely
moving somewhere. Or, maybe it is not. Who is to know? Russia is
growing. Russia is coming back. They are taking over their own selves so
as to one day become a force once again. So there is China, there is
Russia, there is the European Union, there is the United States, there is
Canada, there is Mexico, there is Japan, there is South America, Brazil,
Argentina, Chile, Ecuador, there is India, Pakistan, Israel, Lebanon, and
all of the Middle East. There are Muslims and Christians and all the in-
between. There are people and people with names. People are
everywhere making themselves heard throughout the world. Voices are
singing above the crowd. People are being heard. They are screaming
and fighting with loud missiles of attack. People are dying in the face of
something truly better in the long run.

September 10, 2006

The Economist Magazine is really taking a stance on certain issues in this week's issue. Individual articles seem to be calling out into the world for some sort of action. What sort of action? The kind of action that holds the American police state up at a marvelous degree. The kind of action that says Nazi Germany through the new lens of American police. Homeland Security is becoming one of the most common names, acting as a dangerous proponent and a near fascist form of human control. Homeland Security is the great safety net that blocks all bad things from outside in order to protect the American State and make sure all those citizens are safe from terrorists and Muslims. But have we lost sight of the problem? And what about Saudi Arabia? The Muslims there are our friends. Or at least the state is our friend because we have governmental and business relations with them. But Muslims live there too. Americans may believe war is in sight. War is a very dangerous word, yet people like to use it. War is a very dangerous idea, yet people like to say World War Three is coming. The components of World War Three will have to do with oil, they will have to do with terrorists, they will have to do with Muslims, they will have to do with the Middle East, they will have to do with America, they will have to do with Europe, they will involve China, but China will stay as far away from it as possible, they will have to do with Russia, but Russia will take a stance that is not so great until it really affects the country.

September 23, 2006

The world seems to be getting bored once again. Whenever there is quiet among nations and nobody is waging war on anyone, the world becomes bored and starts to create reasons to indulge in the art of war. Iran is now becoming a highly acclaimed figure. One that requires great attention in hopes of scrapping together a little controversy among nations. Iran is the next big superpower. They are going to be a top figure among others. Iran will live on as one great nation among history. The current big superpowers do not want to see this come true. They are so keen on halting all actions that will bring Iran into the scope of powerful. The current big superpowers are coming together to stop the advancement of such promises. Iran will proclaim however. Why? Because the powers are coming together to try and figure out ways of smothering the competition. Now that Iran knows its influence, the nation will continue to grow. Iran is the one big hope for the Middle East. Then Saudi Arabia. The Middle East will come out of this on top. It shall be known. Germany does not want military interaction. America seems to want military interaction. America will fight. The nation wants it. They need it. From World War Two into Korea, into Vietnam, into Iraq, the nation loves to propagandize war. The people all know it is coming. They all know it is coming. The world says hold on, now wait a minute, but they cannot resist either because the stakes are economically important. Europe is coming together. Russia will stay back as usual until they are needed. Russia is smart and cunning. Japan is somewhere else. Japan is great. They are already in the pure land. The Middle East is getting all confusing in the eyes of the west. This is becoming a mixture of east versus west, Muslim versus non-Muslim, power against power, natural resource versus greedy little hands.

September 28, 2006

My views on Native American land issues have not yet developed. I would most definitely like to know more about the historical and present day happenings of land disputes between Native American Groups and the British (in the past) and Canadians. I have a little understanding of America and Native Americans. I have seen reservations and I know little Native American land or spirit is still present. In Canada there seems to be a recent dispute between housing development and Native American territory. I find it hard to comprehend the pains and destruction Native Americans have faced and must feel from the mass emigration of Europeans. Another issue that is in dispute right now is the water quality within the territories of Native Americans. The water is being polluted and contaminated to such a degree that the people cannot drink it anymore. This must be hard to comprehend. Not being able to drink the water from the stream. What pollution has been created. The same with Hawaii. The people who came from all over the world did not think to take care of the water because people came from the parts that have come to know how to artificially cleanse the water through chemistry and biology. Nobody drinks from the land. Only from faucets. Currently, people can eat some things from the land, but that is likely to change someday.

The Native Americans must be trying hard to live from the land. Their towns / territories are said to be low quality with low quality housing, low quality health care, low quality jobs. This is sad because in my opinion, the Native Americans don't want any high quality social items. They want to live off of the land, but because the land has become polluted, it has become impossible. I can just imagine the British coming to America and before them the Spanish. How they must feel to be driven off of their land. Oh well I guess. There is no more to be said. It is all done with and now everyone is dead and the visions are dead and the myths are dead.

October 2, 2006

America is headed back to where it once was. Until the industrial revolution, which set Britain into the scope of economic success, China and India led the economy. China and India are making their reproach into the lead once again. America is only pretending to be in charge and they are doing it just like other countries did it in the past. It is the only way to stay on top, and it will never end because the minute they stop, their economy will drop back down. I do not think Americans are ready for such low esteem.

I try to think back before World War Two and before America dropped the atomic bomb onto Japan. I try to think back to the ways of America before that because back then I believe America was not as proud as it is now. America was not a global leader. It was its own isolated country.

Things definitely have a way of falling back into their most logical and natural position. The emerging markets of today will cause America to slip. America is not growing as fast as the emerging markets. America is slipping politically and it is slipping economically. What does America have to offer anymore? Nobody trusts America. When did this happen? How did America become such a poorly considered state?

The future will tell a great deal about the current positions of countries. America can only go down, back to its natural position. How America will deal with this is unknown and scary in a sense. I do not believe America will be satisfied with anything less than what it has right now. So, the only thing it can do is go to war. War is the only answer to such a predicament. Look at history and that is what happens. A country grows and grows, then grows some more as it takes a step towards global power. The country flourishes and the people flourish. Then, the country takes a step that it may not have previously taken, but because they are so caught up in the need for growth and their economy depends on it, they have no choice but to wage a war that will most definitely end in devastation.

I cannot see America being satisfied with falling into a lower position than it currently has. This is the danger of America. It must wage war. But on whom? Perhaps on nobody because the world has seen this same scenario in the past. Perhaps the world will consume America's great ambitions without great harm. But then who will take America's place? It will fall back into China's hands, into India's hands, into Iran's hands, into the European Union's hands. Maybe someday Africa will be the great leader of the world. Who knows? Who knows?

October 8, 2006

The world turns. And on and on, the world turns, never able to escape the cycle it turns in. Never able to get passed the simple, humanely needs it cannot seem to take care of, cannot seem to satisfy. Supposedly, China will be the next hero, the next big winner and ruler. America will fall back into the depths of lower apprentice. And oil still turns ugly. And business is running strong through people's veins. Business as usual. The world will be getting rich. America's dollar is growing big. Just like Japans. And how does Japan stay so economically strong? And how does Japan have so much influence on the world? Is it because of America? But even before that, they stood with Germany and Italy. Japan always stays in somehow. But, now what will happen? What will happen as Japan's youth flee the country? What are they preparing for? They are strong in America. They are strong in Brazil. They are traveling outside their borders. They are releasing their women into the wild. What will happen? What are they preparing for? And Africa is the next venture. Business is attacking Africa. Agriculture is trying to stake a claim. At one point, America tried to make Africans in certain parts of Africa rely completely on imported food. This was America's opportunity to Americanize Africa by controlling their eating habits. Africa denied them, but now the Nobel Prize winner says he wants his agricultural revolution to enter into Africa's soil. He wants it to grow in Africa's soil. This means he wants to introduce new irrigation techniques and newly constructed bioengineered plants that resist certain things and grow a certain way. He wants artificially created food to grow in Africa's soil. And the Gate's Foundation is backing him. And another foundation is backing him. Why? Because they see great prosperity through his ideas financially. Africa will be modernized one way or another. Many have tried to do it, but the people just don't grab onto it, but now that the people can see direct results, things might change. Businesses are grabbing hold of the opportunity to earn money through these capitalistic ventures. The world of Africa may change. From the inside. And if the richest people in America are investing in such things, then how can this not happen? Technology is escaping into the hands and ears of the world. Media is escalating. Apple is taking off once again. Apple will continue to grow because they have the leader, they have the money, they have the resources, the engineers, they have the connection, and they have the ideas. Apple will come out with some popular and successful items in the near future. They will come out with some of the most highly bought Christmas gifts that everyone will have. They will come out with the world.

October 11, 2006

Is the world becoming a place of incurable disease? Yes or No? And what is the disease? It is not a bodily disease, although, the body seems to take on the form of the disease over time. Is it a disease of the mind? Perhaps, as the mind is feeding the disease. But what is it? What is this disease that is tearing the world to pieces? It fuels hate and greed, money and power, nation and territory, borders and religion. The disease is life itself, human life. An idea that has been tossed around many times before. Not all humans, but the human machine. The great invisible force that occurs when a large group of people move around within a society. The society has grown to include many people from different parts of the world. This is done through communication. Modern times have made long distance communication possible, which has, in effect, enlarged the social network and social machine. America took a key role in the development of the communicative social network, therefore, I conclude that America took part in building the social machine and therefore took part in building the social machine into the direction it wants or needs. America is not the one to blame however. America alone, no. The world is taking part in this great construction. America may be encouraging, but others are participating, and it is not as if America is the cause of such a devastating rupture, as history shows that this all-conquering prowess has been a function of humankind for a very long time.

October 13, 2006

China has proposed and is now starting to develop an environmental
friendly island located off the coast near Shanghai. This island will not
allow standard gas energy, carbon emitting vehicles. It will use
alternative energy sources for transportation and sustaining the society.
This island will act as a role model for other cities within China as well as
other nations around the world. The economics of such a city may not
work in the end. The actuality of sustainability of the people may not
work out in the end. The point, however, is to attempt this form of living
in hopes that it will work, or at least pave the way for future projects
that are similar. At least, with heads turning towards this direction,
perhaps more money, more research, more education, more devotion,
more politics, more knowledge, could be turned towards this type of
living. Economically and demographically, alternative energy does not
work. It is not beneficial to the economy and large amounts of people
are hard to sustain on the human consumption to energy creation ratio,
but as time passes, as humans always seem to create more efficient
means to the things they have interest in, alternative energy efficiency
could very well become much better. Good enough to sustain large
amounts of people. This is very important when considering the
projected population increase over time. The future will supposedly see
great increases in population. I am unsure as to if the rate in the rise of
population is getting faster meaning the population is growing much
faster as compared to the past. It seems odd to think of the population
growing at any rate faster than it has in the past. People are born and
people die. The longevity of humans may be getting longer. The practice
of western medicine and sanitation may be prolonging the death of the
past generations longer so than previous generations. And, the current
generation may be the longest. Due to this current prolongation, the
population is likely to rise because less people will be dying than
previously. However, the average death age of people will eventually
stabilize and people will die just as they do and have done for all of
time. Therefore, I do not see how the population is rising so drastically.
On the other hand, the rise in population could be caused by the overall
decrease in child deaths that are prevented by western medicine

including surgical performance and the prevention of wide spread diseases. Other factors influencing the population include war, living-conditions, health, natural phenomenon, weather, and the migration of people. The academic world and the world of data show countries, cities, etc. to have massive rises in population. The migration of people could have something to do with this, as well as the expansion of people. One example is North America. When the Native Americans were the only people to inhabit the area of North America, they did not gather in huge numbers of people. They did not multiply in numbers. They did not build cities and grow in population over time. When the land of North America was conquered by people mainly from Europe, the land became inhabited by a large amount of people that were not there previously. The people then expanded and multiplied in great numbers, and they eventually became what is now known as the United States and Canada. This increase in people in these two previously less inhabited areas of land show a direct reason for an increase in population. Then, if taken outwards, these people, who grew in such number went off to marry and reproduce in other parts of the world. The increase in population in one area most definitely increases the population in other areas. This is an amazing phenomenon. However, people have expanded and migrated many times throughout time and history. Why now are the sustainability of people and the growth of population being considered problematic? Is it because only recently have people been able to gather such large amounts of data and data from all around the world? Perhaps the problems are only arising because we are now just starting to look at the world in such abundance.

October 20, 2006

Breaking the words of wisdom. Countries leading toward death. History
has a way of repeating itself, without the clues of people and people's
children. It was not so long ago that the Ottoman Empire ruled the
Middle East and some of the world in the least. It was not long ago
before a shift in power came about when Britain swooped into Turkey's
territory and took control, took away their great Empire. Perhaps
through machinery, through their Navy, through their supreme
strategies and tactics. Whatever way, it happened, and it was not so
long ago. This shift of power seems so far away. I cannot believe it
happened at the turn of the 20th century. How could something so big
not be a part of education? And so we go on doing the same things. No
wonder the people in the Middle East want the United States out. No
wonder they are putting up a fight in their own ways. They have seen
such things before. They know exactly how to deal with things because
they have been through these things in the past, the recent past at that.
Land keeps changing to be owned and ruled by one group or another.
Some countries have rights because of past experiences, past rulings
that are still within their jurisdiction. And the coin turns. It turns and
turns. Africa is a good example. Countries have broken into Africa's
lands and people many times in the past. It is done differently each
time, but it is still done. Africa always seems to be a place that people
go to trying to get their foot in the door, usually through conquering or
for some selfish reason. Right now is no exception, whether through
business, finance, natural resources, labor, and so on. America wants to
help Africa's own people become financially better off by letting them
run the businesses and join the companies; to make it easier and
possible for Africans to own technology such as cell phones and
computers; to create different forms of paying for technology so anyone
can buy. At least some money is being transferred. America wants to
bring lots of aid to Africa in the form of medicine and food. The richest
people in America are pooling their money together for these types of
projects. And so the world goes on and one, like it always has. The next
shift is starting to develop. An era is coming to an end as the old powers
regain their natural composure and power. Sometimes when I think of

the knowledge of the history of people and my lack of it, it strikes me as quite odd that such a lack of the knowledge exists. I am also struck at how just thinking about the history of people and nations make the current world seem ignorant. If these things were done in the relative past, why are people doing them again? Why do terrible things keep happening over and over again, one right after the other? What does it mean that people as a whole cannot learn from their experiences. Such greed. When one nation has power, then other nations must take it from them, but when those new nations get the power, they forget about the old nation and they build up their power more and more until some other nation must take it from them. Contentment is not an option. The forces of evil are strong and they are never going away. Evil looms everywhere, always. Good is hard to see. How are people supposed to give up their great and building fortunes? How are people supposed to give up their great ambitions? There must be some way out of this mess. If only people would believe the history that is so well known. If only people could be content.

October 28, 2006

The news travels far. Communication is a growing facet to society, and society is becoming larger and larger. Soon the world will see a clash of societies. Two or three or four will come up to one another in a heated battle of good versus evil. Everyone has their own interpretation of both good and evil. Everyone will see the other as evil and they will see themselves as good. Oh, it will be a mighty battle. The human race will see grave things. Things so morbid and destructive that their minds will collapse under the extreme pressure of seeing things for the first time that should not exist in life. Life will see things so grave, so destructive like an atomic blast shooting over a civilization. Just like Japan. An atomic blast actually swept over Japan. How grave and destructive. My mind cannot even begin to comprehend the magnitude of such a violent act. People were walking around with their skin hanging off of their bones. The world saw great destructive forces that day. The most terrible things to have ever come about. My eyes begin to water when thinking about such forces playing a role in the current affairs of the planet. This is the most terrible thing to think about. The world collapsing. People seeing the destruction of an atomic blast coming to their home soil. And there is nothing we can do about it, because the forces exist. But then again, people are human and human beings have logic and feelings. They have remorse. If things must play themselves out, maybe there is a chance to play the game of destiny in a fashion that diverts the destructive powers of human kind to once again think in good terms. To divert the forces of evil so we can once again live in complete relevance to social functions without the heat of battle racing down our spines. It is not world peace. Where there is peace there seems to be weakness and someone will always want to overcome the weak, so peace is not an answer. Global understanding of the similarities that everyone has. The world is very similar. It is a similar place. People think in similar terms. Humans are all the same. Understanding ancestors. The economy of human beings. Protect ourselves. We must protect ourselves, not violent protection, but a knowledge of protection that we must protect ourselves from ourselves. We must protect ourselves from ourselves because we possess qualities of utter destruction. Homo Homini Lupus – the human is a wolf towards another human meaning that the most dangerous enemy of humanity is humanity itself. The world is most in danger.

October 31, 2006

Gaining the dollar. Gaining the mind. Companies are growing the dollar. Has there ever been a time in history when so much greed towered over the world? There must have been. I say this because some cultures and social groups have laws and rules that govern their people which make sure greed does not take hold of the people. Some groups of people even have gods that make them realize the destruction of greed. One such law that comes to mind is the law regarding interest rates for Muslims. I have heard that a religious rule says interest rates for borrowing money cannot rise above a certain level. Other groups forbid or highly disapprove taking loans out. And loans are just one example of the greed that affects the world. Some people and companies do not have to take out loans because they have already established their capital, yet they are still trying to gain more and more power and money and influence over other companies even if they have built their capital and they can sustain themselves. What is the great goal of everything, of all of this? When a company grows, the company is successful, yet there does not seem to be any end to the growth. Is this greed? Is this the trick of evil forces? The powers that be may agree.

Virtual worlds. Worlds that are virtual may see greater days. Virtual worlds may be prospective for the future of living a happy life. But even in the virtual world, people bring in their greed and their money. Why does everything have to have a price? People need money, sure. But, how much money do people really need? After reaching sustainability, money is not needed any longer and anything after that is the desire for a better life. Supposedly money makes people happy. I guess so. I am not sure. I cannot say one way or the other. I too crave money. Why? It makes people happy. It is something I would like to have. The virtual world loves advertising. Big companies that are well known and established are entering into this world. Land is even bought, leased, rented, and sold in this world. If the virtual world was, however, to release some of the real world strains on land and people, then the virtual world could be a good thing. For example, if people who crave buying land, crave destruction, crave fighting, crave worldly desires can do these things in the virtual world and spare the real world of their presence, then some good could come out of it. If the virtual world only inspires more destructive events and occurrences and actually trains people in these habits that carry out into the real world, then we may have a problem.

November 9, 2006

There is some inch I am not reaching. Something that the United States
is doing that is making it appear worse off than it is. Or, perhaps this is
my imagination. It seems as if the United States may be pretending to
appear limping along when, in fact, it is stronger than ever. Or, perhaps
this is my imagination and they are slowly but surely falling into
nothingness. Inching along, they seem to be. Where to? Where is
everyone headed, these nations? National unity, business ethics. The
national number one. How is the outcome? What fabulous creatures
deny? I really hope to be spinning soon.

Economic output. Nations wanting talent for their businesses. Nations wanting the brightest minds, putting others in with their golden eyes. The rich get richer and the poor get poorer. National advantageous. National revenge. Whole sale. Whole sailor.

The pieces are so only pieces. How does one begin to see the world with more of a keen eye; more of a truthful eye? The population is populated. These people are people in numbers. Some liked to be ruled. Some like to rule. The figures run out in the manner that they do. Economics is key. Business and fortune are key. The world is coming together in the wrong fashion. People are dangerous. People are safe. The world is moving along, but where to? And why is the world moving along? Who is pushing it? Is it some invisible hand drawing people in, scooting them along? I am just not sure. What right does one have to say such a thing? The pieces are so only pieces. The world is made up of pieces. We can now buy those pieces with a fortune. That is all it takes, just a fortune. Then people will use their fortune. And some have it without fortune. It is just the way of life. Either with money or without it. Money or none, but always the same thing. Always a hand at the base of it.

November 13, 2006

Progress of many nations. The progress of governmental power and positions does not seem to be progress at all. Rather than developing and growing in a beneficial or mindful manner, the progress of governmental power and positions goes round and round in a circle of the same destructive and mind-boggling manner. When viewing democracy as a single component separate from all other forms of government, it may seem very healthy and good for the people. When viewing democracy as an offspring of forms of government in the past, it may seem to be a good thing for its people and those people around the government, who inevitably become effected by the government of democracy. When looking at the direction democracy is headed and when viewing the way democracy is being pushed and pulled and how the leaders of the democratic government are using democracy to push their own ideas, then democracy seems to fall into place alongside all of the other forms of government that have somehow failed and come to pass throughout history. Humanity is composed of many different people with many different agendas. The agendas are the same cross-culturally. Those people, whose agendas bring them to attain power and lead nations, fall into whatever form of government is in place at the time, or whatever form the world will soon have after encountering these people with the agendas to attain power. The turn of the world always goes round and always comes back to the same place, which is fine, but ignoring that phenomenon by pretending the current world is the most sophisticated and is on the right path of righteousness will cause destruction. Democracy is becoming just like every other form of government that is now looked upon as bad. This can be demonstrated in many different ways. One way to see this is through the different nations and their respective governments. Democracy is a fairly new form of government. (The democracy of today) Before democracy, the prevailing government was the government of fascism/communism/national socialism. These were the governments that led nations into battle during World War Two. It seems odd to think that so many nations, including Germany, Russia, Italy, and Japan all took on similar forms of government and all turned to violence and destruction. The pushing upon others is not the government but the people in power within the government. Now, the pushing people are leading the democratic struggle. They are invading nations and instilling the democratic government that the nation's people run. Democracy is going to dissolve eventually. When the time comes for a new government to rule over the majority of the people and nations in the world, democracy will fade out just like the others. It seems hard to imagine, but someday, democracy will be looked upon as evil just as democracy looks down upon communism and fascism. That is hard to imagine, but the turns democracy is taking show this quite clearly. Democracy in its righteous form, in my opinion, would not venture off into the world and invade, conquer, and reintegrate itself onto other nations and people. That is not democracy. That is the people using the power of government to fulfill their own agendas.

Agendas reach far. They reach deep. Humans cannot avoid their agenda and there is nothing wrong with fulfilling your agenda, even if it is bad and leads to terrible things. The discrepancy is ignoring it or pretending it does not exist and using the world to fulfill the agenda without acknowledging its existence. When this is done, the human is not acknowledging their own existence.

November 16, 2006

The company as an entity. An entity as in relation to a nation, a
governmental body, or historical era. The company is the new nation.
Just as nations are a relatively new entity, the nation with borders and
specified as a nation, the company can take the place of the nation
without borders, yet existing in the virtual borders of the nation it
originates from. Alliances are beginning to develop. Alliances between
nations. And with alliances comes opposition. Where one alliance
comes together another breaks apart. With opposition comes the
potential for action being taken to insure a winner, and with every
winner there is always a loser. Not only are companies creating alliances
with other companies cross borders, cross nationally, but companies are
moving their offices into other nations. Some keep their original
nation's ties; others become completely new entities existing within the
new country's borders. Takeovers are becoming more and more
evident. Now one nation can actually takeover another nation's entity.

The company is a great way to bring nations together. People are now linked better than before and the company makes living abroad easy and readily available. The company can be taken into many directions. This is similar to the internet, as most companies exist within the virtual world as well. The company can become a magnificent connection between peoples. A way to communicate ideas with other people. However, the direction it is starting to take, similar to the direction other entities have taken before is the direction of wrong-doings. The same situations have occurred in the past, the only difference is they were done with violence. The company is more theoretical, existing through money and figures. As long as the company stays theoretical then people will not be injured through violent acts and reactions to being taken over or taken advantage of. The moment when the company defies law in the form of violence, then that is when people will see a change to the world. Law is a great controller for these entities. It tries to control the wrong-doings, but it does not work for everything, as some companies take the risk of getting caught because the profit succeeds the loss taken through penalties of law. The other problem is that of who creates the laws. As the world comes together and the companies all play the same type of economic game, then they are going to have to follow the same rules. These rules are slowly but surely creeping into every nation taking part in the company world. I have heard from a man working in Switzerland that the United States has implemented global laws that are affecting the way the Swiss run bank runs its affairs. Certain guidelines must be met. Global laws are also a good way to create global awareness and come to compromises between nations and peoples. This is a good way to understand different people. However, just as companies can take bad directions, laws, the creation of laws, and the way they are handled can also take bad directions. Power and prestige seem to lie at the base of all of this. People strive to become bigger and bigger with no end in sight. Even the biggest entities strive to become bigger even though it is nearly impossible to become bigger, but where else are they going to go? They cannot strive to become smaller. And staying stagnant creates economic problems. Just as nations and eras in history sought to become bigger and expand their borders and power, the company is doing the same thing. But once again, as long as the company stays virtual and theoretical, the forces will act themselves out without violence and destruction because just like eras have come and gone in the past, the company era will dissolve sometime in the future, being replaced by some new type of power and control.

November 23, 2006

North Korea has supposedly done a Nuclear Bomb Test. This supposed test has created much tension in the air for the world's leaders. What to do about North Korea's actions is looming on the minds of many nations including the United States, China, Japan, and South Korea. For many, there is nothing that can be done. For others, decisive action seems to be the response to the test. Many factors come into play when deciding what to do about the test. The hopeful thing is that everyone has at least been thinking about the consequences before acting. People are talking, however cruel and threatening those talks may be. At least they are talking. And each nation has their way of thinking and talking. It shows a lot about the nature of the people and the history that has come into play. China's true knowledge comes into play during these pressure filled moments to calm the situation and play a daddy figure to the world. In such times of heat, China seems to know how to deal with the situation. They are tolerant and know the dangers of acting out of control. One view of the situation shows that North Korea must stay as it is in order to continue the balance of population and social design between North Korea, South Korea, China, and Japan. And, if North Korea were to collapse, the question of what would happen to the nation comes into play. Would China swallow it as their own? Would the Koreas unite? Would the United States put up a fight to have ownership or at least have precedence and presence? The migration of people into China is put into thought. The number of nations with nuclear possession is growing. The number with nuclear potential is growing. Inevitably, the world will see nuclear ambitions in the future. The cold war is taking over the world. Powers are growing. Nuclear weapons are becoming the staple for power. Tests are being conducted. Sanctions are useless. The voice of America is dwindling. Someday soon, the United States will become just like North Korea: a fading power reaching for attention. When the moment comes that the United States wants to be recognized and listened to, but nobody cares, that is the time when the U.S. will act out in frustration. This frustration is already developing. The U.S. called for action in Iraq and the world listened and watched. They paid attention and respected the decision. But because of its failure and dragging out with nothing to show for, the world is no longer listening. The world could have turned many different ways, but because of the path it did take, the consequences will play themselves out as another moment of history when things can be looked upon with uneasy eyes. Why? Why did it have to happen that way? And so it goes. As the world transforms over and over again. The world of immigration and migration continues. Power shifts. People shift. The next fifty years are beginning to develop. The nations of the world continue to grow and fall. And some stay the same just as they always have because they know the ups and down of life. The comings and goings. Some people see beyond the bickering of the present age and see the age as all of time. Some people see it all.

November 27, 2006

Telecommunications. The technological future of communications. Companies are really into it. The network of the future is being built and companies are getting ready to deliver all of the goods and services that will be introduced in the future and that will be integrated with the new network. The big expected future network of the past failed the telecommunications companies. They prepared and spent lots of money on the future market, but failed. This can happen again, which is why companies must be careful and move slowly and surely one step at a time. The telecommunications industry is combining different types of media, components, technology, and services all in one package. An example includes television, cable, internet, and phone, all in one. The network these companies are creating is the network that can handle everything. I can imagine the network having better mobility as well. Mobile remote access and/or wireless capabilities. It should be global, but global is hard right now because different countries have different companies running their telecommunications industry and therefore every country has different interests. Overall, I would say the success of the telecommunications will be the manipulation of people to enter into their market. How many people will the telecommunications companies get to pay them money for goods and services? People do want this stuff anyway. The companies will not be forcing people to buy these things. People will already want them. In fact, companies are going to look for the things people want most and cater to their wants and needs completely. For some companies, they will be able to advertise to such an extent and degree, that they will be able to implant their product into the minds of people so people crave their product without having wanted or needed it in the first place. This is with many things of today. The world is filled with things and services that are all inventions of man for the purpose of doing things that are also creations of man. The world is now a creation of man. But even though I talk down upon the world as a creation of man, I must take part in it, and I must enjoy it because if I do not enjoy it I will fail in my own attempts. I will study the telecommunications market and I will look at the stocks of those companies that are in the telecommunications industry and more specifically, I will focus on the companies that are currently small and unknown, but are taking a risk by developing the network and products of the future use of telecommunications. This is a risky play; however, at the same time, I will also focus on the big companies that are well established and are investing in the future market, so hopefully, they will balance and not only balance, but balance in a profitable way. I will try not to take part in the manipulation of people. This means I will try not to hope for the success of the ideas of the company just so I can make a profit. I do want to make a profit, but I will try to hold some morality. I want to be an active, passive participant. If the new telecom industry develops then good, I will have successfully made a future prediction and saw it go as I thought. It will be interesting, none the less, to see how something develops over my lifetime. These are the trends of my lifetime. In the past it was something else, and now it is this. Over the next fifty years, I will see how the economics of the world develops through trend, through products, through services, through information, and through the market. By using my intelligence, I should be able to take part in the advancement of such industries and invest money in those industries now to watch them grow on into the future. People of older age must be more aggressive because they do not have as much time to watch the advancement of the market. These are the people leading the way. Perhaps they will burn themselves out before reaching any paramount idea that revolutionizes anything. When the paramount finally does come, it seems as if it has passed already onto some bigger and better idea or future potential market. The world is never satisfied.

December 8, 2006.

The sudden slowdown in the housing market is tough to decipher. I will only be able to judge by my own experience. My family has put a condo onto the market probably at the wrong time, but if the slowdown is only a slowdown and not a stop, then time may surely bring people to buy a condo at market price. If nobody buys, my family and I will sit on the property and wait for the next turn around in the market. The sudden slowdown seems to be getting much attention from the world. That is the slowdown: special attention, information, and opinion creating the slowdown. Media has a huge impact on the happenings of the world. Media can determine what people will do and how they think about certain issues. Media is a very powerful tool. The opinions of those who are creating the content or approving the content are very influential thus very powerful. People will listen to the media and start making decisions based on the media's content. That content will act as the basis of a decision. The decision will be justified by the media, saying that it is truth. Currently, the media's content is leading the world into a specific direction: America seems to be taking a slow descent while Asia ascends. America may be headed downward. But, what really is going on? America is testing its power. Yet other nations are not taking to it as they might have in the past. Perhaps many people do not see the downfall of America thus they will continue to buy. But the media is so loud. The price of housing has hit its peak for this go-around and the media has made this clear. People definitely realize that they can buy for less: the buyer's market. Many sellers, not so many buyers. Our condo is worth more, but we are selling it for market price and that market price may seem high if the buyer realizes that if he or she waits, the price for a similar condo will fall. We are in bad shape. The potential for growth in the price of the condo is strong. Some people may see the potential growth and act on it. However, if America continues down the route it is currently taking, I am afraid America's economy will drop down and not return to its current state for a very long time. Specific events must happen for this to come true, but history tells a clear story that it is possible. In recent history, America has fallen and risen and fallen and risen, so this may just be another reoccurrence.

December 15, 2006

Turkey is turning into a tremendous entity in my mind. It holds so much knowledge, prowess, capabilities, history, diversity, controversy, and compromise within itself. The people within this country happen to fall on both sides of the global division of religion, nationalism, and opinion. The east meets west within at this great piece of land and social structure. Turkey is magnificent. And now it is torn once again between its calling to be distinguished as a western entity or an eastern entity. This division is set to the beat of joining the EU in its formulation, meaning compromises must be met, and disputes regarding neighboring Greek Cypriots; or denying joining the EU and staying its independent self; or taking the side of the Islamic headstrong and holding onto the culture and traditions it has kept for thousands of years. When viewing Turkey, I cannot help to think of the great history which has bestowed upon this planet a great knowledge. The nations and people that have conquered the world. Khan of Mongolia. This great figure who's legacy introduced this people to the world, but who lives in quietude now. The world is waiting for the next conqueror to step forward. People will slowly begin to see, but maybe not for a long time and maybe not until something devastating happens. But Turkey. This great and powerful country is taking shape. They are now making decisions. Oh, how I must know more about the Ottoman Empire. This quiet mark in time.

December 22, 2006

The boundaries that exist between peoples are constantly changing. I remember learning that the many nations were created very recently in time. The nation with its borders and government is quite different than the nation with its culture and language. They do become intertwined, but the distinction does exist. This learning was through the perspective of pre-world war Europe. The development of the state. This state having to do with the nation. How the people living inside the nation were forced to comply with the state. How a government and leader took control of the state and set itself against other nation states. The nation state is drastically changing right now; however, because the changes are occurring through the hidden agenda of finance and the borders are staying as they were, the change is not evident. Rather than explaining the details of how it is working through companies, countries, and financial institutions, I want to stay focused on the line of thought that groups of people, nations, and what is considered a nation or state are all constantly changing and what exists right now is only temporary and it is very different from what existed in the past. The nation is so real to people of this time. The boundaries that enclose a nation state are very real. Maps make this evident. Although, different groups of people living under different nation states most likely have different maps. As companies originating from different countries settle into different countries, the clarification of who they are becomes fuzzy. Their place of origin composes some distinctions that make it reflect the nation it came from; however, that company also adapts to the country it settles in, taking on characteristics of that country's people. It must, otherwise it will not be accepted and in effect, it will not make money. Companies and financial institutions take over other companies and financial institutions all of the time – countries and nations become indifferent. One component of the company versus company that is arising is that in some nations, companies are run by the government. In this sense, the stakes become upped and thus there is more potential for nation intervention through the government. For example, if a water company in country A takes over an electric company in country B, both run by the government, then what is so different than country A taking over country B in terms of government as opposed to company? What is so different about country A taking over country B through government intervention than country A's company run by the government taking over country B's company run by the government? The cover up is too good. Thus, the cover up is too dangerous. Some people probably do not realize the severity of these interactions. The company is a created entity, just the same as nation states and borders. At the time of origination for the nation state and borders, similar takeovers occurred as are occurring now through company. Money is the key difference. With money together with laws and regulations, takeovers usually happen with both parties agreeing. Company A may let company B takeover their company if the stakes are high enough. Money equates to power. But why takeover? Big, successful companies must takeover in order to survive and continue to grow. Why is this? No reason other than it is inside the human spirit. Humans love to takeover and conquer, thus the success of companies lies in the same manifestation of human social structure. I do not think people realize they are the ones creating the direction things such as company interaction take. All social interactions are created by human. Too bad most of it is unconscious. Too bad the most influential people and the ones with most driving force are the ones in power who are taking social interactions into these morally wrong routes. Taking over a different entity meaning taking over a different people is not a wise thing. It always leads to destruction. How far will these takeovers go? The day will come when a government will intervene with violence.

January 4, 2007

The template of the world is taking shape. U.S. in Hawaii is taking shape. It does not really exist. Hawaii has accepted the customs and culture of the U.S. Someday, the U.S. will leave the island, and / or, all of the people living in Hawaii will return to the customs and culture of Hawaii without the interference. These days will surely come.

Today, I learned about a small war between China and India in 1962. That amazes me as China and India are both very powerful and influential. Such wars happening today would most definitely be high tempered and have high consequences.

The United States played influence on Iraq in the hanging of the ruler Saddam Hussein. He was tried in a court of law in Iraq and sentenced to death by hanging. He was killed on December 30, 2006. What will happen from this? Maybe nothing. Maybe the world will pass it by in hopes that no violence or war erupts from the event. But, the event will surely live on as an historical event, looking back upon the event as the time when the United States invaded Iraq and the Middle East, overtook the government, emplaced and influenced a new government which tried the captured leader for genocide and sentenced to death.

The world may no longer view the United States as a good example, as the example. The world is taking a new shape. People want a bit of change. China and India are regaining their control. Russia is regaining its dominance and self-sustainability. Obama may gain a seed as the next democratic runner over Hilary Clinton. The people of the United States will hopefully not be fooled once again by the presidents. Or, at least, this generation, as the past has seen things similar that this generation never learned. The problem of forgetting causes more problems than just forgetting. Repeating things that should not be repeated. Making the same naïve mistakes over and over again without ever progressing. Or, people will never attain their ideal utopia. People will forever live in cultural difference due to hatred and fear of the other. People will never be satisfied. People will always try to take over and conquer. These things exist as virtues within the human being. They cannot be discarded. Sorry.

January 13, 2007

The day brings new developments in world history. The state seems to be taking more control. American State. Policy forces are heavily enforcing the State's laws, and more importantly, they are enforcing America's set of values and social regulations. That is the funny part. The laws and enforcement of laws is one thing and the other enforcement is that of American values and social norms. For example, parking at a parking lot. When parking at a parking lot, one should follow the arrows and abide in a manner similar if not identical to the manners that an American would comply with. If the manners do not match that of an American, then a police enforcer is likely to turn his head and think about what he could do to remedy the situation, perhaps with a ticket. Laws are mere replications of values. America's values must be so strange to other people. And for people to have to use force and the identity of a police officer to make sure people follow those values and way of life seems strange. Why should someone have to force another to follow a culture's set of values? Should they not be engrained in the mindset of the person? This is scary. Maybe because America is such a young country that is pretending to be older than it really is. Maybe America is corrupt. Maybe America has been keeping the Native Americans locked up concentration camps. Maybe America is trying to rule the world. Maybe America is taking over other people and similar things to past and other conquerors. America is working hard for something that is for sure. It is working hard and spending the earnings of working hard on military defense and military attack or advancement.

America is heavily populated by police force. Much more than some countries that seem to be heavily enforced because of their governmental stance. But America is scary how enforced it is while at the same time preaching freedom and democracy.

I can only imagine it getting worse too. How could it get better? What turning of events would occur to make it better? The only turn of events could be a catastrophic event such as a war or violence. America may be drowned out and fade away, but I don't think that will stop the enforcement of social norms and laws by the police state. I fear for the future of America. It already seems to be showing signs of weakening through the financial dollar and the financial outlook through stocks and related things. I sense America's destruction in my life time. Surely, a big change of events will occur in my lifetime. All of the signs are beginning to show. Racist Islamic and Arab, Middle East remarks. These are happening all over the world. Capitalism getting mixed in with politics and democracy. Capitalism taking a wrong path. Countries growing strong after the failings of World War Two. America becoming more aggressive. But at the same time, America about to take on a new president who could racially change things.

The future of the world is uncertain, but one thing for sure is that the future is merely a replication of the past. Nothing new has been gained. History only repeats itself so long as the young are not made aware of what occurred and so long as people try to forget because of financial gains.

www.ingramcontent.com/pod-product-compliance
Lightning Source LLC
Chambersburg PA
CBHW051817170526
45167CB00005B/2058